EXTRAORDINARY BOSTON

1st Overleaf: Rowing shells, Charles River, Cambridge.   *2nd Overleaf:* Beacon Hill at dusk.

Edited by James B. Patrick.
Designed by Donald G. Paulhus.

Printed in Singapore
through Palace Press
LaJolla, California U.S.A.
ISBN 0-930527-07-0

First Printing, 1986
Second Printing, 1987
Third Printing, 1989
Fourth Printing, 1990

Published by Foremost Books,
a division of Embassy Imprint, Inc.
Old Saybrook, Connecticut 06475 U.S.A.
1-800-999-1075

EXTRAORDINARY
BOSTON

Photography and text by Steve Dunwell

Published by Foremost Books
A division of Embassy Imprint, Inc.

EXTRAORDINARY BOSTON

This is a special place in America. Here, at the confluence of powerful natural, historical, commercial, and cultural currents, a unique metropolis has risen, sculpted by these forces and expressing their interplay. This is a city with resonance. Here the new is wrapped around and overlays the old without obscuring it, creating contrasts that enrich urban life, engage the mind and delight the eye. Transformed by imaginative and audacious enterprise, this city has become a dramatic metaphorical landscape. Modern towers challenge venerable monuments. Ancient enclaves persist within new districts. The Cradle of Liberty is ringed by the Nursery of Commerce and the Trade School of Architecture. Here the citizens of this narrow peninsula converted a good harbor into a great city: Extraordinary Boston.

Connoisseurs of Boston are the beneficiaries of this remarkable heritage. Every view reveals an aspect of transformation. Any walk through the city cuts across history like an archeological dig. Panoramas from roof tops or from the air provide new prospects on these juxtapositions. The higher the point of view, the more clearly the new encircles the old. The same sunlight which glances off cobbled streets and granite warehouses also blazes on the glass and chrome of adjacent towers, making an inspiring American landscape.

Early settlers used the Shawmut Peninsula much as they found it – setting a beacon on the highest hill, establishing their town on the flatland by the cove, and grazing their cattle on the Common. But this acceptance of natural limits was short-lived. Even before the Revolution, the waterfront was reshaped with wharves, dams, forts and seawalls. Two decades after Boston patriots tossed British tea into the harbor, Boston developers began shearing hilltops and dumping their gravel into the same harbor, starting a process of expansion and redefinition which has produced the city we see today.

Ambitious landfill became the theme of Boston development. Since the new buildings which colonized the new land used the latest styles, the expansion of the peninsula created a concentric history of architecture and urban design. Periodic fires and aggressive demolition wiped parts of the landscape clean, allowing new design to infiltrate the ancient Hub.

Charles Bulfinch set the tone for the city which expanded onto this altered landscape. He placed an elegant domed statehouse on John Hancock's hilltop pasture and designed stately symmetrical homes for the gentry on the slopes below. At General Hospital and along the wharves, his designs in granite are the acme of Federal style. At Quincy Market, his followers confirmed this early standard of excellence and imaginative design by superimposing long granite arcades on the run-down and ragged town docks that preceded it, creating a grand ceremonial entrance to the city from the harbor. More than just fine buildings, these designs establish urbane public spaces which characterize Boston.

From these auspicious beginnings, a parade of great architects and planners have designed new urban environments for the expanding city and superimposed them on the previous landscape. Louisburg Square was laid over the sheared hillside of Mt. Vernon. Ropewalks at the foot of the Common were cleared to make room for a grand Public Garden. The salt meadows of the Charles River were filled to make the South End, the Back Bay, and a new shoreline for Cambridge. On the dusty plain that became Copley Square, H. H. Richardson set his masterpiece – Trinity Church. F. L. Olmsted transformed the Muddy River swamps into the rustic Fenway and designed an Emerald Necklace for the remade peninsula.

The filled lands between the Public Garden and the Fenway became a showcase of Victorian style and energy. This was a prosperous and creative period for Boston. Lowell's power loom, Singer's sewing machine, Ames' ploughs and Gillette's razors made this a manufacturing center whose vitality continued even as the China Trade declined. Boston drew talent and invention like a magnet. Immigration brought new social pressure as the population doubled every decade. The citizens responded with a Grand Urban Experiment to transform the peninsula.

Now the Back Bay, the South End, and parts of downtown rebuilt after the Great Fire of 1872 are treasuries of architecture – on a grand scale and in ornamental detail. Richly articulated bay- and bow-fronts ripple down long axial streets. Mansard roofs of myriad patterns provide a rich and varied crest to the sturdy brick blocks which march west from the Common. South End streets are relieved by quiet oval inlets at Union Park, Worcester Square and Chester Square.

The treasury of Boston buildings offers a world tour without leaving the peninsula. A Florentine campanile marks the skyline along with English church steeples. Replicas of a Petrograd bridge, a Venetian palazzo, and a French boulevard enliven the landscape. Every district has its Greek temple. Egyptian lotus columns grace selected entries. Exuberant stylistic vitality enriches the city. The South End has its Cyclorama; Back Bay, its Second Empire mansions. Teutonic castles guard the entrances to India Street and to Columbus Avenue. Tiled pyramids top off skyscraper ziggurats. Allegorical figures and historical bas-relief educate the pedestrian about the cultivation of tea, the principles of navigation and the virtue of Industry.

By the turn of the century the transformation was almost complete. Between the Institute of Technology on the north and the Esplanade on the south, the Charles River became – at high tide – a reflecting pool for Beacon Hill. The waterfront expanded until its radius equalled Long Wharf. Similar wharfing-out converted Noddles Island into East Boston and Dorchester Heights into South Boston. Warehouses and manufacturing lofts surrounded the vestiges of Fort Point Channel. Radiating from the Hub, the streetcar suburbs of Jamaica Plain, Brookline, Brighton, and Roxbury were relieved by Olmsted's Emerald Necklace of parkland, ending – in concept – at Castle Island, now joined to Southie at the tip of Marine Park. Citizens of Boston admired the trees of the Arnold

Arboretum and strolled the pastures of Franklin Park.

During this century of expansion, the Boston skyline was marked mainly by church spires and chimneys. The most dramatic vertical accents were the granite obelisk atop Bunker Hill, the eagle-topped shaft Bulfinch placed on Beacon Hill, and Boston Light. Standing beside the Old State House, the thirteen-story Ames Building was the city's tallest office block. The skyline kept this low profile until 1913, when a thirty-story Art Deco tower was planted above the rotunda of the Customs House. This dramatic landmark ruled the skyline for a half-century, setting a new standard for audacity in design – the new right on top of the old – that previewed the great skyscrapers which followed. Over the freight yards of the Back Bay, Prudential created a new family of towers. Beside venerable Trinity Church, Hancock angled a monumental glass obelisk. Scollay Square was erased to make room for Government Center. Copley Place vaulted over the turnpike corridor. Only two blocks from the Customs House, Exchange Place updates the concept with blue glass walls soaring over the old granite facade. At nearby Fort Hill, International Place rises where both fort and hill have vanished.

The new glass and steel towers have transformed the Boston skyline as forcefully as the preceding landfill remade its perimeter. Confined by a High Spine concept, separated from sacred residential districts, these skyscrapers march in an articulated column from the Fens to the Hub, massing there in a concentrated upthrust of commercial energy – a simplified metaphorical promenade of enterprise approximating the original peninsula.

With its spine of new towers, Boston packs dense urban culture into a small place. Walking from the edge of the Fens to the tip of Long Wharf takes only an hour, yet covers three centuries of civic invention. Indeed, among the great delights of Boston is the miniaturization which local geography has enforced. The transformed and layered cityscape is challenging, yet comprehensible. It is small enough to know, yet rich enough to reward continuing study. Though packed with skyscrapers, the Hub is still only minutes from the Common and the harbor. Any random stroll samples many diverse environments.

This is a city which rewards the pedestrian. The citizen can perambulate the Hub, study its variegated texture, and contemplate its history. Walking through Boston, one can sense more easily the spirit of the intellectual giants who occupied the Hub before the corporate towers muscled in. Daniel Webster and Horace Mann guard the State House. Park Street Church still echoes with Garrison's abolitionist zeal. Emerson, Longfellow and Whittier can be imagined on the streets of Beacon Hill.

From high-rise offices, the citizen can survey broad panoramas. The exercise of imagination and the limits of creativity become clear. Only the aviator sees more. Viewed from above, Boston reveals its transformed topography. As altitude increases, the outlines of the peninsula and the harbor emerge. Architecture recedes into texture as the developer's hand clearly dominates. Historical relationships between Boston, Charlestown, Dorchester and Cambridge become visible. At the highest altitudes, the encircling arms of Cape Ann and Cape Cod come into view, dramatizing the shelter and opportunity which distinguish Boston Harbor.

Like the obelisks of Stonehenge, the towers of the Hub and the grid behind it record the changing seasons and shifting angles of light. The Bunker Hill monument serves as a giant sundial for Charlestown. Radial avenues dramatize the solar calendar. Watch the summer sun as it lights the Old State House at dawn and turns Summer Street warehouses to dusky gold. Behold Commonwealth Avenue in October as the setting sun shoots along its rippling facades. See the harvest moon float up over Beacon Hill. Winter sunsets transfigure South End avenues. At Copley Square, the Hancock Tower reflects and intensifies both light and weather while measuring the days with its shadow. As spring approaches, a celebration of magnolia blossoms surprises the Back Bay. The city comes alive with dramatic light.

The views collected here distill the impressions of a Boston enthusiast. First as a visitor, then as a resident, I have learned the resonance of this special city. These images preserve the wonders of discovery that make learning fun. It's only a short walk from my door to the Public Garden, and as I turn onto Arlington Street, I sense the marshy tide flat that it used to be. The brick sidewalk even seems a bit more springy. Arriving at the Garden, I marvel now as I did when I first saw it – an oasis in this brick enclave, graced by stately swanboats. Standing between the Doric columns of the Custom House, I can see the bowsprits of clipper ships moored in front and imagine Hawthorne hunched over his ledger inside. Climbing Copps Hill, I look across to Charlestown and see Paul Revere waiting.

Photographs can freeze special moments and angles where all elements are optimized. Too often the view flashes by, as the city seems to do when seen from commercial aircraft on take-off or landing. Before the traveler can say "Look at the light on that building!" the moment is gone. These photographs intend to capture some of those fleeting glimpses and crystallize them for future study. Through views of the city we understand better its underlying principles.

Boston is a taut web of urban vitality. Unique among American cities, it has the range and depth of history on display. Lines of influence link Old North Church to Bunker Hill, Old Ironsides to Boston Lighthouse. Commercial energy crackles between the Customs House Tower and the Hancock Tower. The quest for enlightenment joins the spires of Park Street to Harvard Square. Bronson Alcott described this as a city "upon which the light of the sun of righteousness has risen." To our amazement, his claim was not entirely arrogant. Boston is, indeed, illuminated by a special light. As the sun clears the horizon by the nation's oldest lighthouse, it shines on a tiny gem of urban imagination set in a dramatic harbor of history. Poignant and hopeful, the Hub glows in the dawn.

Steve Dunwell
Boston, Mass.
January, 1986

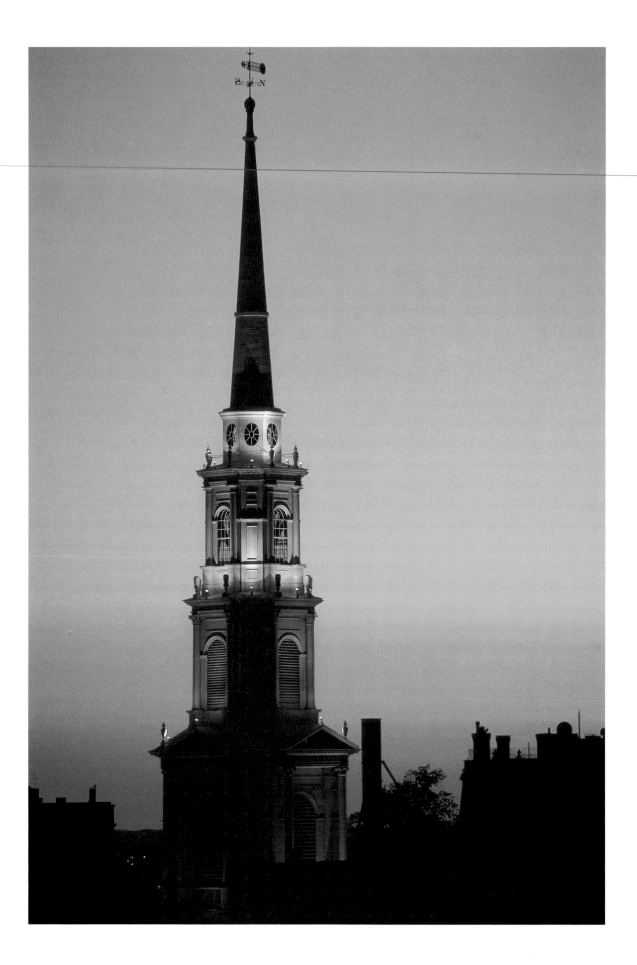

Park Street Church, 1809 Spire

John Hancock tower, Back Bay to Dorchester Bay

Freight yard skyline, Brighton

Turnpike toll station, Allston

Boston Post Building, Milk Street

Customs House tower, State Street   *Overleaf:* Storrow Drive, along the Charles River

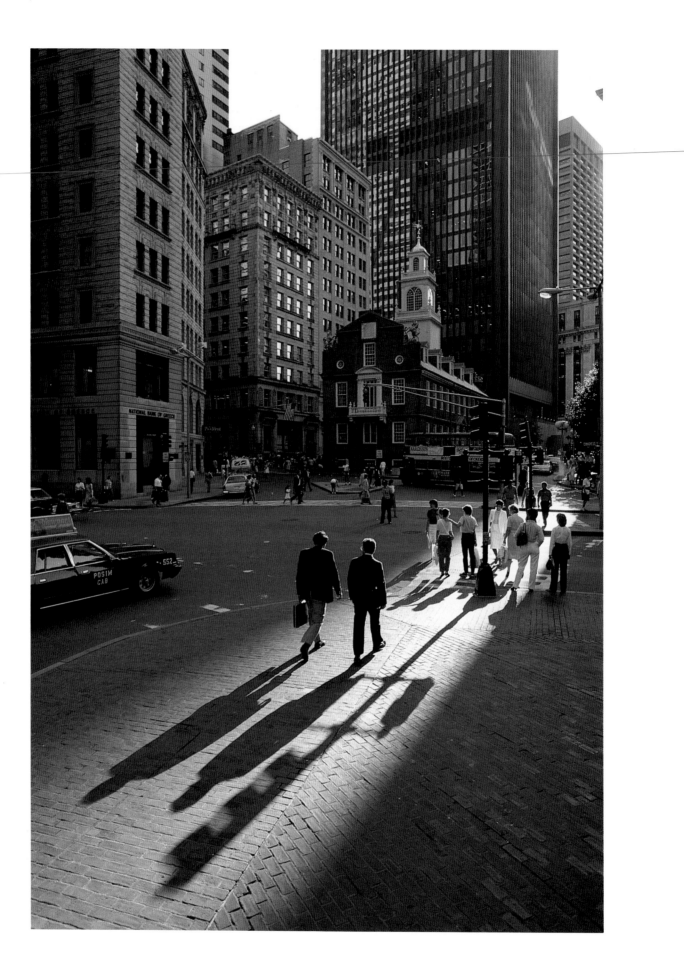

The Old State House, State Street

Federal Reserve Bank tower, Summer Street

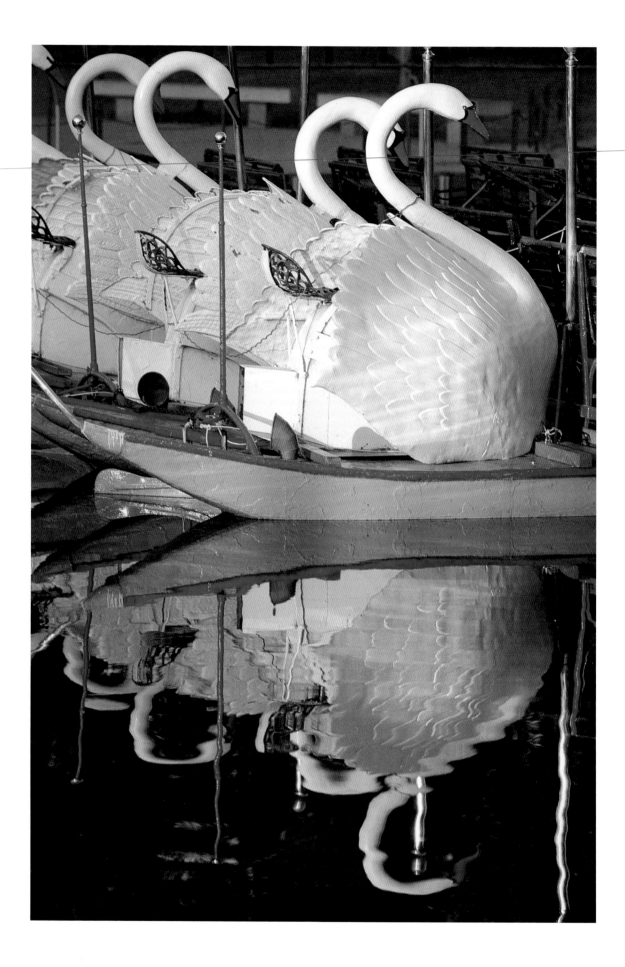

Victorian swanboats, Public Garden

Spring afternoon, Public Garden

Frog Pond fountain, the Common

Corinthian columns, State Street

Overleaf: Beacon Hill skyline, Boston University boathouse

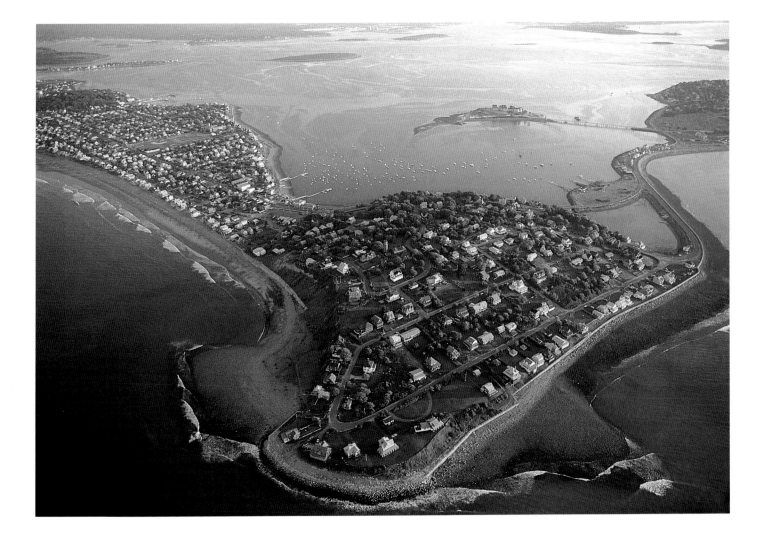

Inner harbor, East Boston

Nantasket peninsula, Hull

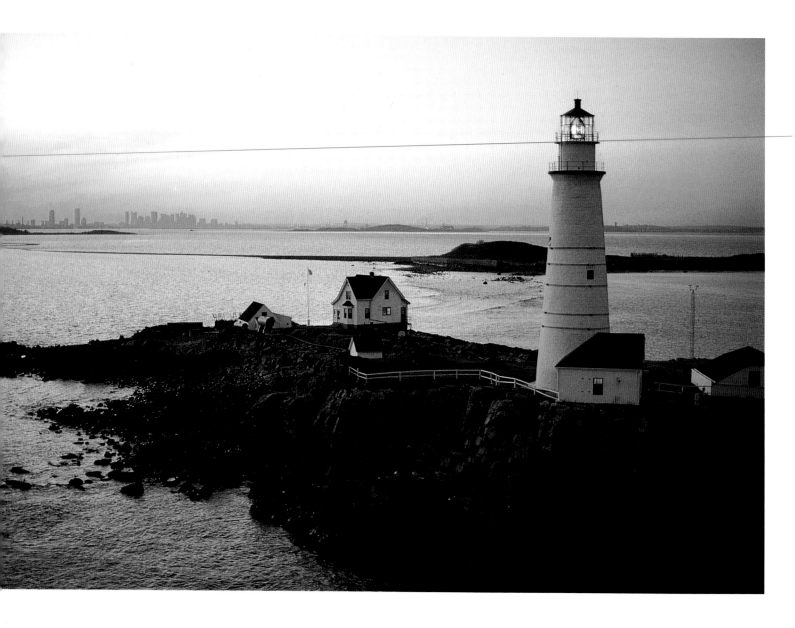

Boston Light, Little Brewster Island

Back Bay evening, Community Boating

Overleaf: Bandstand, Crescent Beach, Revere

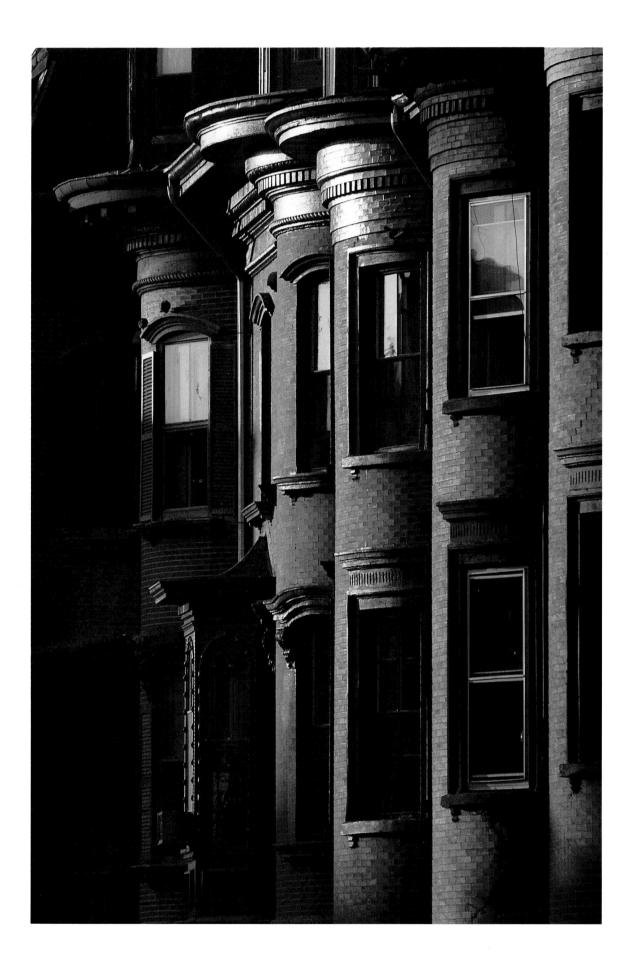

Church of the Advent, view towards Cambridge   Chester Square bowfronts, South End

Dorchester Heights monument, Thomas Park, South Boston

Chester Square, Massachusetts Avenue

Trinity Church, Copley Square

Old North Church, North End

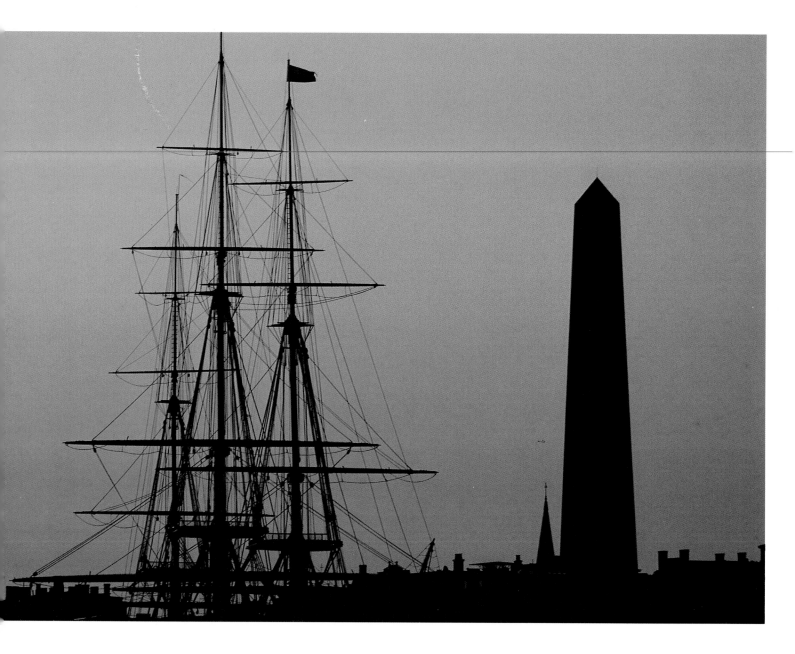

U.S.S. Constitution rigging, Bunker Hill, Charlestown

Clam diggers at low tide, Revere Beach   *Overleaf:* Public Garden and Boston Common, from the Ritz

Mother Church, Christian Science Center   Crosswalks, Boylston and Dalton Streets

Lilacs on Bussey Hill, Arnold Arboretum

Three-decker houses, Dorchester

Overleaf: Financial District, from Harbor Towers

Two Hancock towers, Back Bay   Evening with ducks, Charles River Esplanade

Family garden, the Fenway

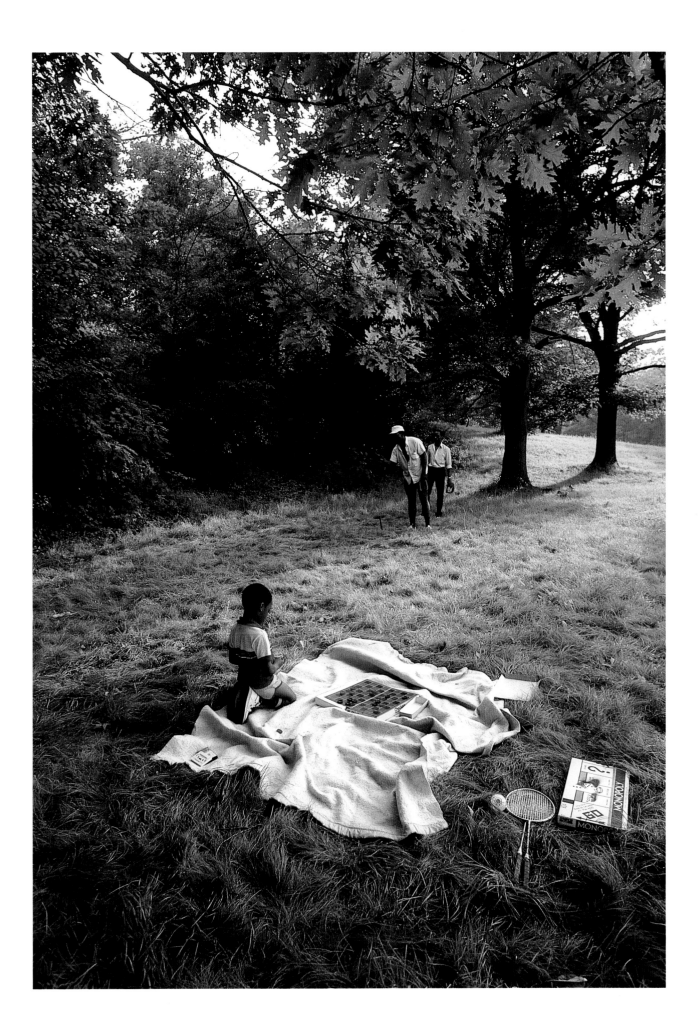

Summer picnic, Franklin Park   *Overleaf:* The Isabella Stewart Gardner Museum courtyard

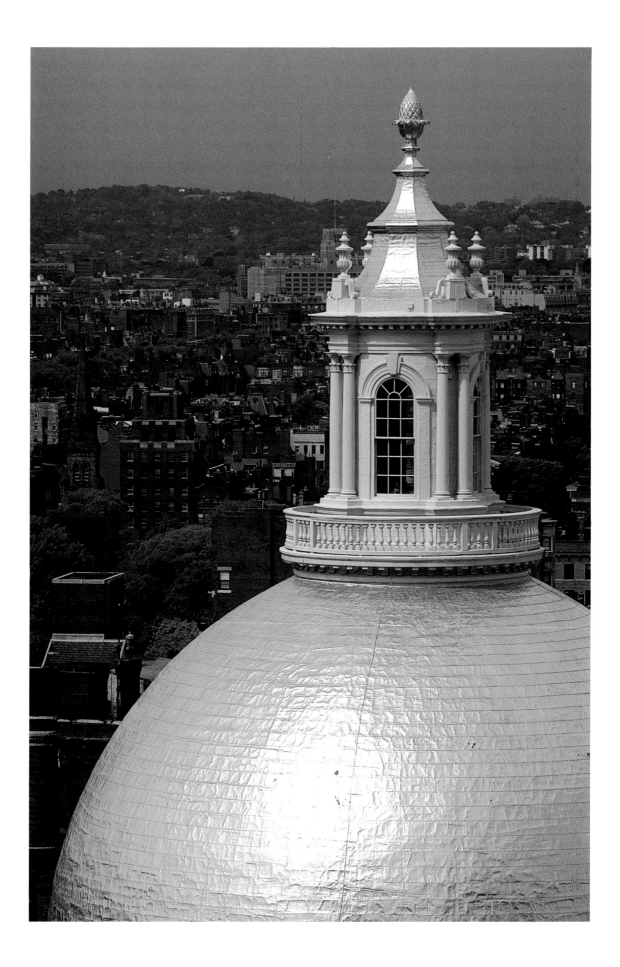

Hancock Towers and Trinity Church, Copley Square   Gilded Bulfinch dome, State House

Jamaica Pond, Jamaica Plain

Beacon Street, Boston Common autumn

Overleaf: Back Bay skyline and Longfellow Bridge

July Fourth fireworks, Boston Pops at Hatch Shell   Turnpike taillights, the Back Bay

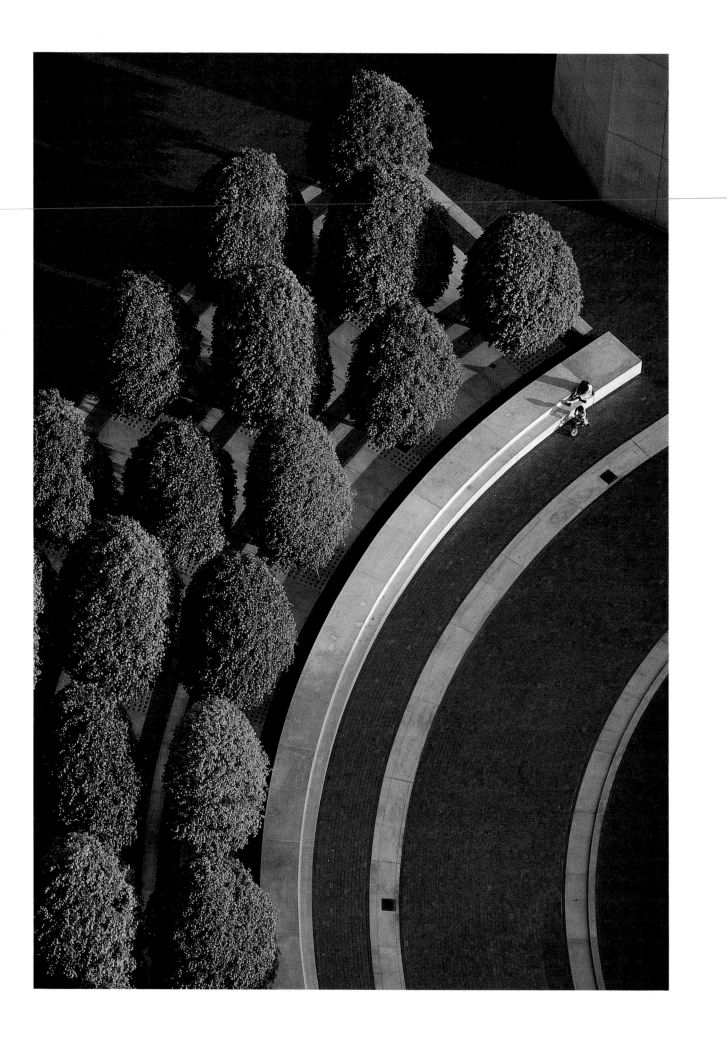

Spring afternoon, Christian Science Center

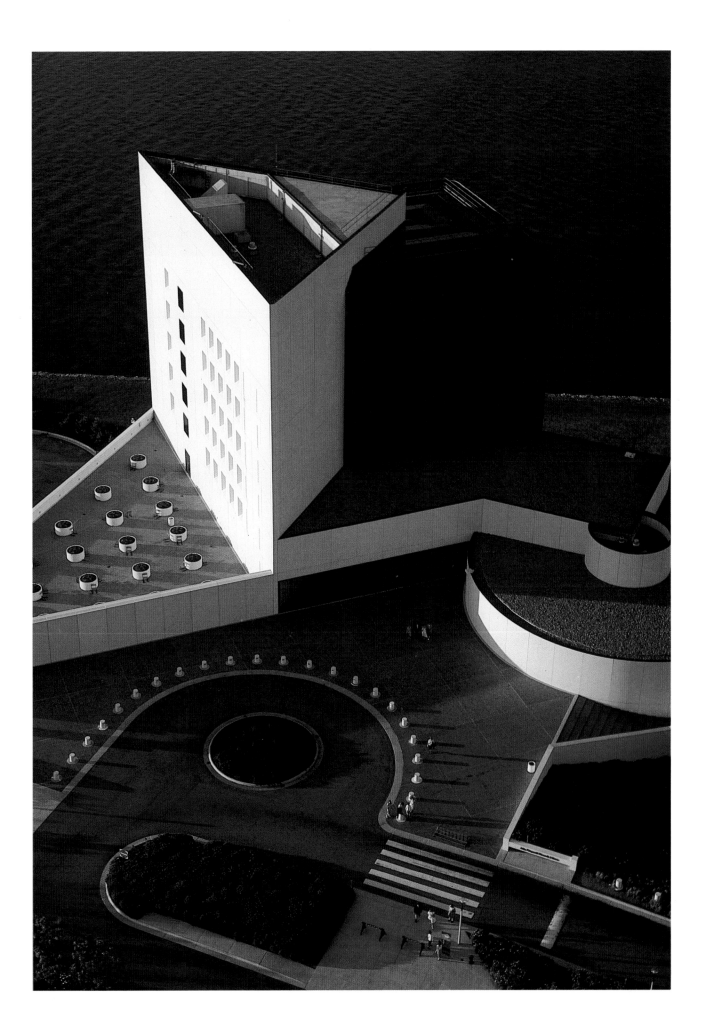

Kennedy Library, Dorchester Bay   *Overleaf:* Tulips encircle George Washington, Public Garden

Magnolia blossoms, Commonwealth Avenue

Mount Vernon Street, Beacon

Public Garden and Boston Common, downtown   Springtime crossing, the Public Garden

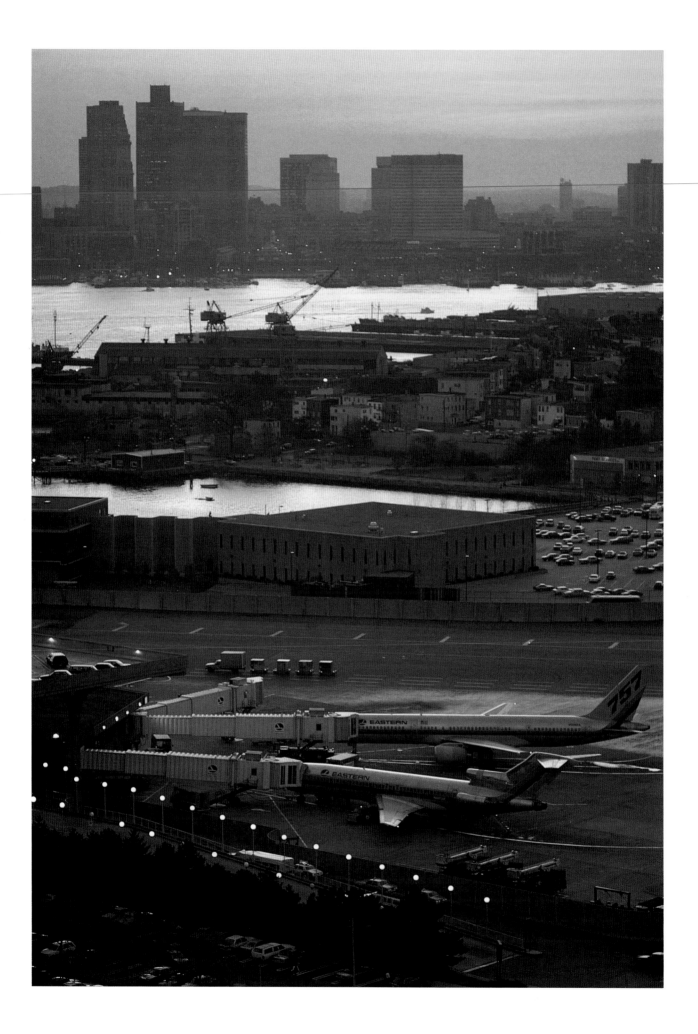

Harbor at dusk, from Logan Airport tower

Harbor at dawn, from East Boston

Overleaf: Rowing at sunrise, Charles River

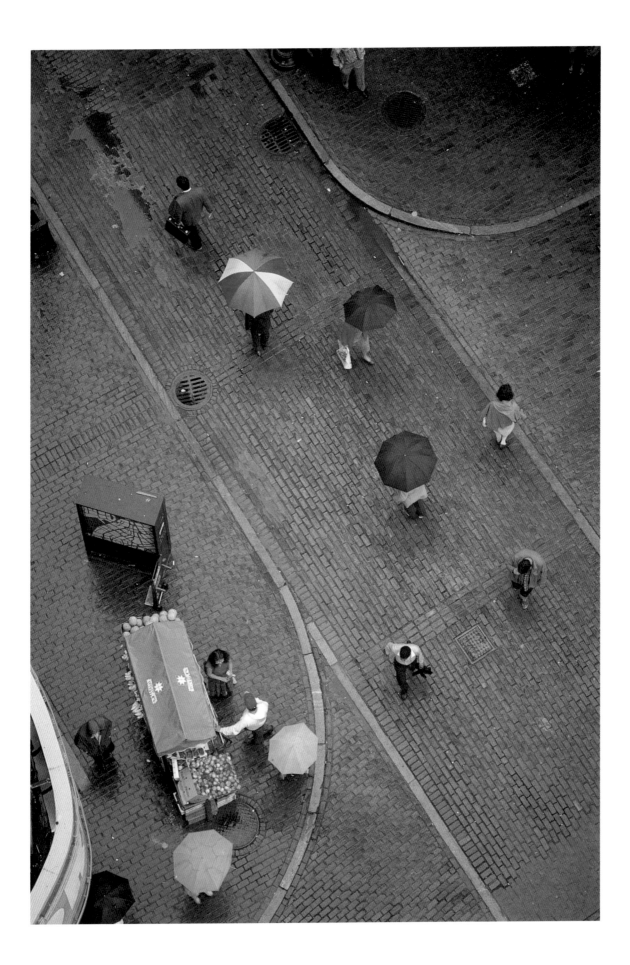

Quincy Market and Faneuil Hall, Dock Square   Washington, Summer and Winter Streets, downtown crossing

Trinity Church

Back Bay to South End panorama, from Prudential

Overleaf: Museum of Fine Arts

Bunker Hill Monument, Mystic River Bridge   Park Street Church, Tremont Street

Quincy Market and North Market

Beach Street entrance, Chinatown

Moran container terminal, Charlestown

Tugboat piers, East Boston   *Overleaf:* "Holy Hornblowers," First Baptist Church, Commonwealth Avenue

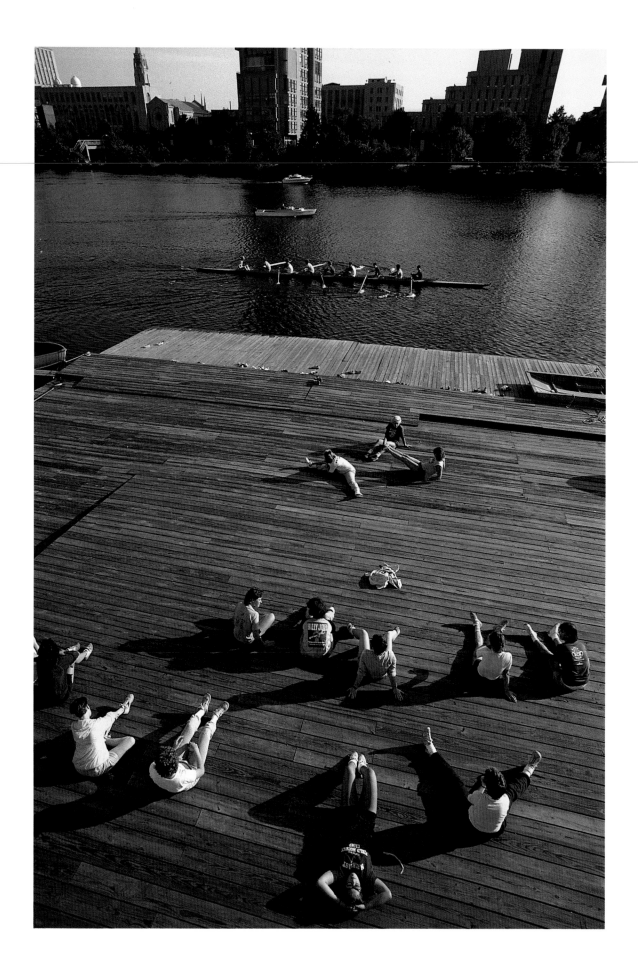

Women's crew exercises, Boston University   Community Boating dock, the Esplanade

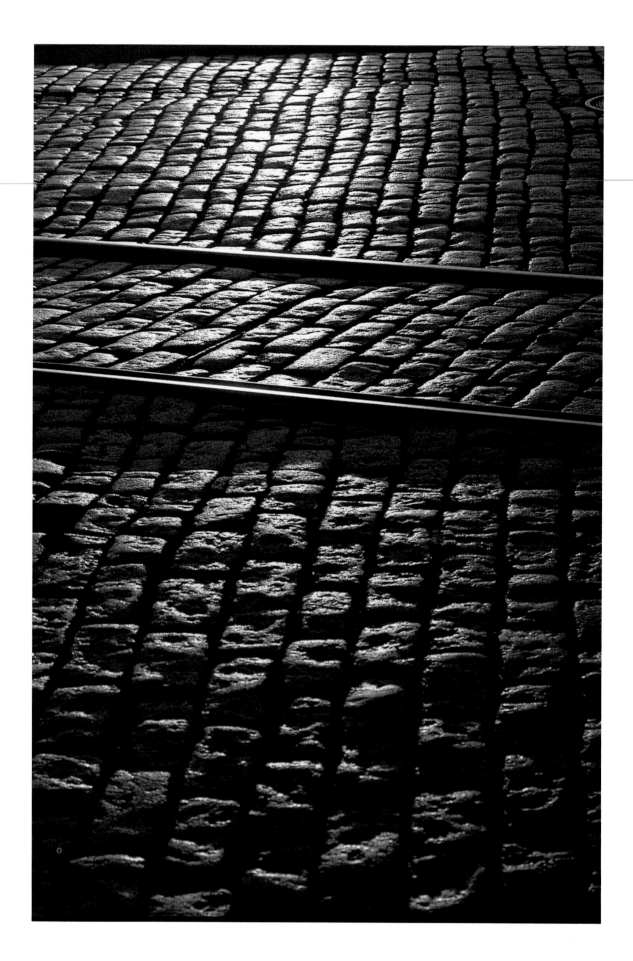

Tracks and cobbles, Northern Avenue, South Boston

Lofts and warehouses, Summer Street

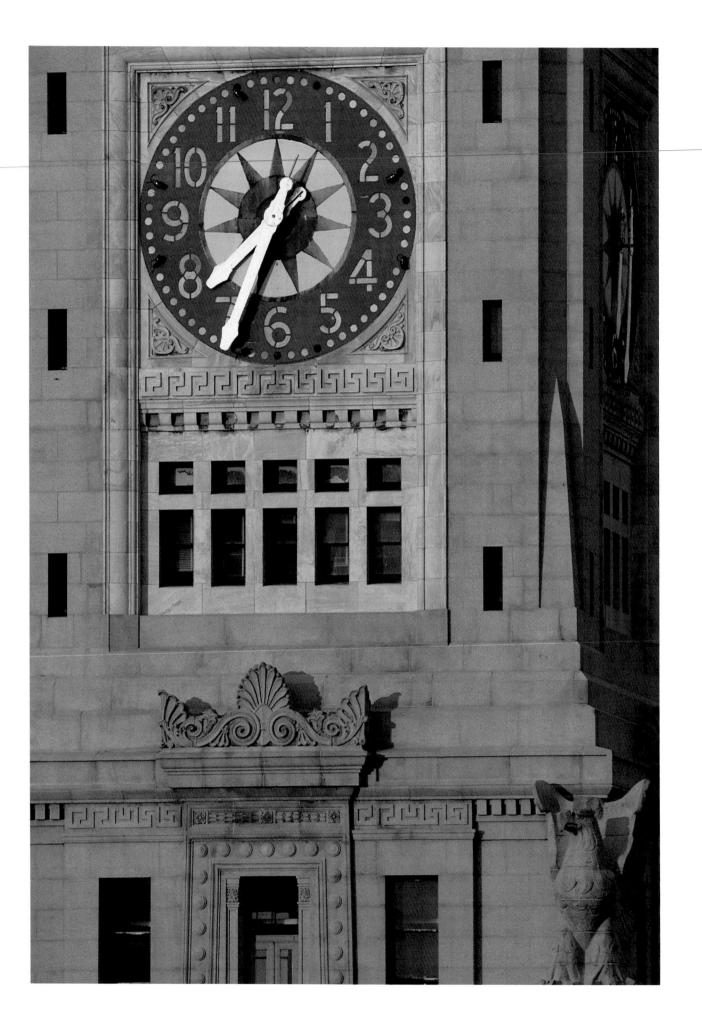

Clock tower detail, Customs House

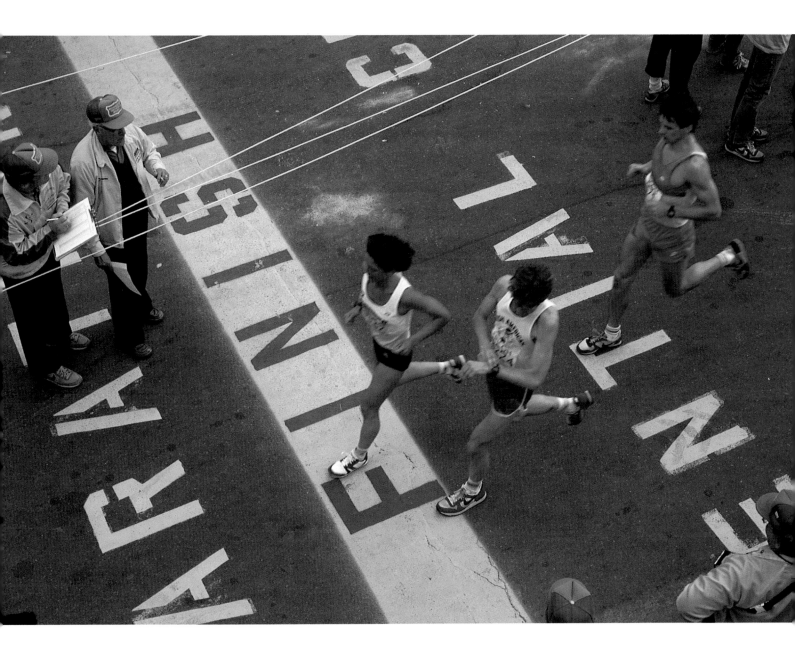

Finish line, Boston Marathon

Overleaf: Downtown at dawn

The Boston Celtics, Boston Garden   The Boston Red Sox, Fenway Park

Harbor Towers, Grain and Flour Exchange

Summer evening by Longfellow Bridge, Charles River

Overleaf: The Old Granary Burying Ground

Sixty State Street, from Exchange Place   Crosswalk, Summer Street

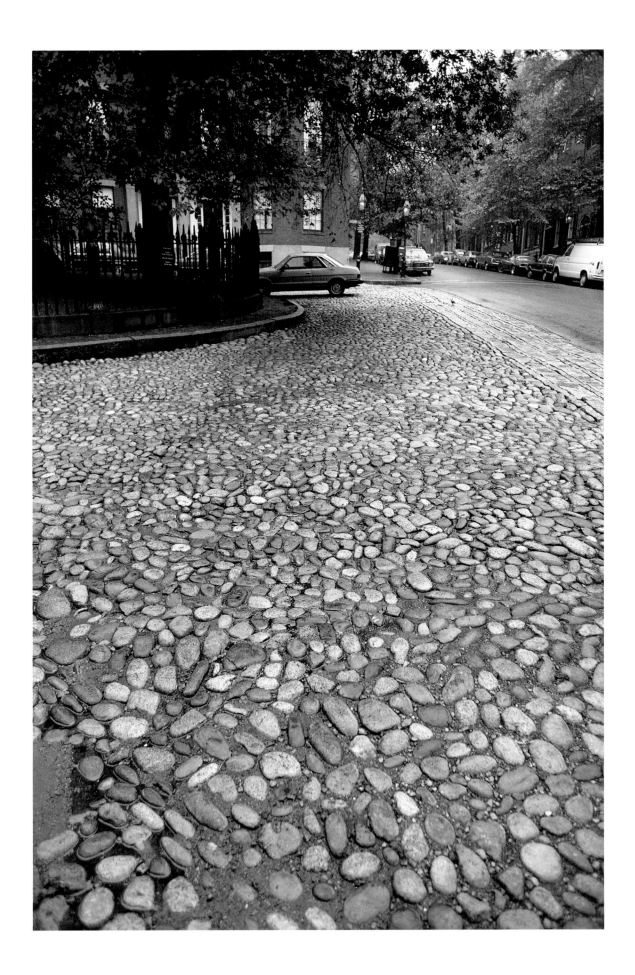

Cumulus clouds over Park Street

Louisburg Square cobblestones, Mount Vernon Street

Swanboats at rest, the Public Garden

Overleaf: Harbor sunset, from Hull to Boston

Saturday morning shopping, Haymarket Square   Festival of St. Anthony, Endicott Street, North End   *Overleaf:* The downtown waterfront

Overleaf: General Joseph Hooker statue, Beacon Street   Community boating, Charles River   Beacon Hill, State House, downtown dusk

Monument Square, Bunker Hill, Charlestown   Fort Independence, Castle Island

Salem Street, North End

Newbury Street, Back Bay

Evening panorama, Deco to Modern

Overleaf: Boston, Nahant, Marblehead, Cape Ann and beyond